This Notebook Belongs To

Made in the USA
Monee, IL
05 December 2021

83968926R00070